MW00881758

How To Create A
blog

blogging
for beginners

Blogger Versus WordPress Blogs

by Jazevox

Legal Disclaimer

Table of Contents

Introduction - What Is Blogging?

Blogging Then. During its early stage, blogging used to be a means to write an informal journal or diary in order to chronicle a blogger's day to day personal activities, to document personal experiences and be able to share these updates online mostly with family and friends.

A blog is a convenient way to keep family and friends, especially those who live far away, updated with what is going on in a blogger's life. It is a great way to stay connected and informed with the regular activities and happenings of a blogger's life even if love ones don't live together in the same roof.

Many bloggers utilize blogs to share their family activities, life updates, travel experiences, group adventures and gatherings, etc.

Blogging Evolution. Although, there are still a lot of bloggers who blog for personal purpose, blogging has evolved way more than that nowadays. Blogging is not solely being used to share personal experiences as many individuals also utilize blogging nowadays as a way to share their knowledge or expertise in a particular subject or niche. Even though there are still several bloggers out there that utilize blogs to write about their personal journeys, blogging is certainly no longer limited to this purpose alone.

Many blogs nowadays are great resource of information for several different topics reason being is that many bloggers have been utilizing the blogging platform to document several different type of topics or niches, for instance, crafting projects or advise for job hunters, etc. There are numerous individuals who utilize blogs to voice out their views and expertise about certain topics, share their opinions or reviews about particular products and/or services.

In recent years, many businesses utilize the blogging medium as a way to document or give information about their products and services. Blogging is now commonly being used by many businesses or companies to inform their clients or customers as well as the general public about certain company updates and announcements or any other information that they would like to share publicly.

Blog Post Specification. There are no strict specific rules what you can put or write in a blog post, or how long a blog post should be. You can have as short as one or two paragraphs blog entry, or as long as you want. You can add pictures and images, or none at all. You can even have a wordless blog post, just post pictures or images, or even just an embedded video is considered a blog post.

As a blogger who owns your own blog, you have the flexibility and complete control of the type of content and the quality and quantity of content that you publish in your own blog.

But if you are blogging for a business or a company, then you, being the representative of the company and posting blog contents on behalf of the company, might have to follow certain standards and criteria in all your blog posts to ensure that you keep the company's integrity intact and its reputation secured considering that anyone or anybody can just publicly read whatever content you post in the blog. So you have to abide to the specific blogging and publicity guidelines set forth by the company who owns the blog, whose reputation is on the line.

The company who owns the blog may require you to follow specific format, style, or approach in all the blog posts that you publish. Specifications and guidelines varies depending on the company itself.

Blog Versus Traditional Website. You are probably wondering what is the difference between a blog and a traditional website?

Although a blog is also considered a website, a blog differs significantly from a traditional website because of the way a blog is presented and how its contents are normally arranged. A blog is a series of posts or articles arranged in a chronological order, usually by date basing on when each blog post was created and posted in the blog.

Whereas in a traditional website, majority of the contents or other pages of the website are access through a navigational menu or clickable links, and the pages are not necessarily posted by date but usually by topic or categories.

Most notable visual difference is that a traditional website usually have the navigational menu (usually by topic), as mentioned above, in which the site visitor can click to explore web pages within the website, whereas a blog usually don't have such clickable menu, but can optionally have one too. Instead, a blog usually have a clickable archive list of all posts normally arranged by posting date.

Blog Maintenance Overview - Do You Have What It Takes?

Let me ask you this, before you jump into a swimming pool, wouldn't you prefer to know the temperature of the water first? You will never know the temperature of the water just by looking at the inviting sparkly crystal blue water.

Same goes with blogging! It is definitely wise to know in advance what it takes to maintain a blog. Are you really up for it? Are you really willing to do this? These are things you need to assess beforehand, before you spend anymore of your precious time because as you go deeper and deeper into blogging, it's only going to take more and more of your time and suck in a lot of your ideas.

If you are planning to operate a blog, you need to assess yourself, preferably in the beginning of the process, to know if you have what it takes to do this long term. Since there are so many moving pieces when it comes to blogging successfully and have your blog thrive for a long time. It is important to know what it takes to keep your blog going so that you will be able to sustain it for several years since blogging is a long term commitment. If you have the desire to blog, I don't think your vision is only to do it for few years and then abandon it, right? I'm sure you envisioned your blog to last for a long time.

Granted, blogging will take a lot of your time, you might as well know beforehand what it takes to maintain a blog and see what you are up against to see if this is truly something that you want to do. Once you have some bird's eye view and have some ideas on the tasks ahead and what needs to be done, then you can better prepare yourself, be better equipped, get ready and move forward with blogging.

One major challenge of blogging is being able to produce contents in a consistent basis. The way in which a blog is presented online, which is in chronological order, it is so easy to determine when a blog is updated regularly or not. The way blog works is that the latest blog post, by default, is usually displayed on the first or top page of the blog. So when someone visits your blog, the blog visitor can easily tell when the blog was last updated, basing on the date of the last post which is usually the first post the visitor will see when he/she arrives in your blog.

Although it is highly advisable that you post in a consistent manner, there is no fix rule as to how frequent you should update a blog in order for it to be considered regularly updated.

Originally, many bloggers blog on a daily basis. Daily blogging might be easier to pull off when you are blogging about personal experiences since most people don't run out of day to day activities so there is always opportunities to blog about. There is always something going on in people's lives, doing this, doing that. All of these stuff they do are all potential blog posts.

However, if you are blogging about a specific niche or topic, it is a completely different story. Sometimes, you might need to do additional research in order to provide accurate, valuable and informative information about the topic. Writing a blog post on a daily basis can become overwhelming overtime and can cause burn outs, and burn outs can cause lack of enthusiasm and motivation.

By choosing to blog every day, you will soon realize that you are running out of ideas to blog about.

Just remember that there are 30 days in a month, that means 30 blog post ideas that you have to come up with in order to blog on a daily basis. Do you have 30 blog post ideas right now? If so, then great! You have one month worth of blog posts!

Many bloggers nowadays prefer to update their blogs on a weekly basis, as this blogging frequency seems to be so much more manageable compare to daily postings.

You can, however, post daily if you have the capability and the drive to do so. As mentioned earlier, there is no fix rule how frequent you should post. It is your decision to make.

You may be up for the challenge of daily blogging but then you have to also consider your readers. How often do your readers really want to read your blog? Do you think that by posting daily it will encourage your readers and followers to check your blog constantly, as constant as every single day? Or it will become overwhelming for them and therefore could benefit more from a weekly blog updates instead of daily updates.

It is also good to take into consideration that most people are busy with their own lives, therefore they might not have as frequent as everyday to spend reading your blog diligently. But then again, everybody is different, so you have to consider that although some readers may have time to read daily, some may not. The answers to these vague unknowns also depends on your target demographic.

Ultimately, it's all up to you to decide if you should do daily blogging or not.

Because of the nature of how a blog works, as mentioned earlier, which is usually arranged in chronological order, it naturally demands consistent updating, not necessary required, but doing so is a huge contributing factor for the overall success of your blog in the long run.

Consistent blogging does not mean daily blogging, it can be blogging at certain day of the week and keeping at it every single week.

To be a consistent blogger, it will demand a lot of your time and energy, and most importantly a lot of your creative ideas on what to blog about, that's why it is important that you are highly passionate about what you blog about (will be discuss further in the next chapter) because you have to constantly come up of ideas related to your blog on a regular manner for as long as you keep your blog alive and going.

When you are highly passionate about your blog niche, you have much better chance of coming up of plenty of blog post ideas and not ran out of it pretty quickly. You will need at least one blog post either weekly, bi-weekly, or whenever, depending on the frequency of posting that you decided on.

Can you imagine if you do decide to blog daily? How long do you think you can sustain your blog with all your existing blog post ideas if you decide to post on a daily basis?

Let's say you have thirty (30) different ideas of blog posts for your blog. And let's say that you decide to blog every day, what will happen the next month? Can you come up with the next thirty new ideas to write about related to your blog? What about the month after that? And so on and so forth.

This is why it is important that you determine your posting frequency ahead of time because you can visualize how much inventories of ideas you have available, and how fast they will ran out because your supply of ideas will go down either slow or fast depending on the frequency of your posting.

It is also important to point out that being able to produce blog contents on a consistent basis encourage your readers and followers to check out your blog regularly because you are giving them that impression that you do update your blog regularly and they can rely on the fact that when they do re-visit your blog that they can expect to see a new blog post.

Even though you don't announce your regular posting schedules, your regular readers can judge the timing of your postings by seeing the date intervals in between your posts. If you follow certain posting schedule, then your regular readers might start to notice certain patterns or sequence in your postings, for instance, you usually post unannounced every weekend, or every Tuesday, etc.

In cases that you are unable to update your blog consistently as you would like, there can be not-so-desirable effects and consequences that can occur. Imagine one of your blog follower visiting your blog one day and noticed that your last post was from three months ago. She might give you a benefit of a doubt and visit your blog again the following month, and if she sees the same old blog post that she saw the last time she visited, then that could cause some uncertainties in her mind, and she might make that dreaded conclusion that your blog is not updated regularly, or worse, that you are neglecting your own blog. With the conclusion that your blog visitor draw on her own, she might decide that from then on she will no longer visit your blog. Multiply that head count to all your regular readers. That can be a devastating loss of followers that you worked so hard to acquire from the start.

With that said, blog needs consistent updating, but to do so, it is so much easier said than done. I have to admit, as a blogger myself, it is not easy to come up with new blog posts regularly. I personally ran out of blog ideas on several occasions so I also face so much challenges trying to keep my blogs up-to-date on a regular basis.

As mentioned earlier, there is no fix rule as to the frequency of your blog posts, you can choose to update it daily, weekly, bi-monthly, or monthly, etc. But whatever posting frequency you decided on, it is highly advisable that you stick with that frequency in order to develop regular readers and followers in your blog, and they will feel that they can rely on your posting sequence and be confident that when they expect to see a blog post in that day of the week, they will. It may sound harsh and demanding, but this is one way to keep your audience reading and engaging with your content on a regular basis.

In order to develop regular audience or readers in your blog, you need to provide valuable up-to-date blog posts on a consistent basis for as long as your blog exist. That could mean several years, or perhaps a lifetime? Yes, it sound like work, but that is the type of commitment that you have to realize early on before you even make a decision to start a blog or not.

Whether you like it or not, a blog will certainly demand this type of maintenance for as long as you are blogging. The question is, are you up for it?

What To Blog About - Finding A Blog Niche

DISCLAIMER: There are some portions of this chapter that contains excerpt from my other book, How To Make A YouTube Channel. So if you happen to read that book prior to this one, that's why some paragraphs may sound alike because of trying to explain the same topics without the inconvenience of referring you or sending you to another book. It seems more convenient for the reader if I just insert such information in this book directly.

One of the most common challenge that many bloggers face today is what to blog about. So if you are one of those who are struggling to find the right niche to blog about, keep reading.

Finding the right niche or topic for a blog always seems to be the first hurdle that many people struggle to decide when they create a blog. But it is an important process because you need to be able to visualize ahead of time where your blog is going in the future. You need to see the bigger picture so that you can slowly put the pieces together, one blog post at a time. By doing this, you are building a strong foundation for your niche-specific blog.

By having a clear vision of what your blog is all about and how you see your blog in the future, you can then start mapping out your plans early and act on those plans diligently in order to progress towards those goals and reach the level of success that you envisioned for your blog.

Part of mapping out your blog plans is coming up with blog post ideas. Blog post ideas are dependent on your blog niche. Therefore, the sooner you can figure out your blog niche, the faster you can start planning you blog posts, and build your blog, one post at a time.

Finding Your Niche. To make the process simpler for you when finding the right niche, think of the things that you are passionate about, the things that you love to do on a regular basis.

I strongly suggest that you don't just jump into a niche that you know nothing about or you are not into it, simply because you observe that many bloggers are doing it.

For example, there are many bloggers that are blogging about beauty and makeup (as an example for the ladies). But if you wear makeup once in a blue moon then it might not be such a good idea to write about makeup since you have limited knowledge or hardly no experience about the subject.

It is harder to preach something when you do not live the lifestyle nor do not do what you preach. I mean, you can, but it will take you a lot more time, energy and effort to write those type of blog posts because you also have to do additional research and figure out the niche itself, aside from constructing a blog post.

A great way to start in finding the right niche for yourself is to ask yourself some of these simple questions:

What are the things that you love to do?

What are your hobbies?

What are your interests?

What keeps you motivated and going on a regular basis?

It can be anything, really. Pets? Health? Exercise? Music? Playing instruments? Technology? Real estate? Business? Design? Arts? Crafts? Giving advice or helping others?

One great thing about blogging is that you have the option to choose whatever topic works best for you that you are comfortable writing about.

The best part about blogging is that you are pretty much your own boss, you run the show and you have the control and the power to choose what you want to write about, it's entirely up to you, except for the illegal and prohibited topics like pornography, hate crime, etc.

Why Finding The Right Niche For You Is Important. A blog is your center stage, with potentially the world as your readers or audience. So your creativity and imagination will play an important role in how well you present your blog, one blog post at a time.

Whatever topic you blog about, people who are passionate about the same topic, or are going through the same thing you go through, basing on the stories and experiences that you share on your blog, they will be able to relate to you more on a personal level and they are more likely inclined to follow you. You will develop a following if you put up enough valuable contents that your audience can relate to.

One of the main reason why it is so important that you have to consider the things that interests you and what you are truly passionate about is because it will give you the ability to produce better and more believable contents on a regular basis long term because you love doing it, you enjoy doing it.

Your readers will be able to tell when you are passionate about your blog. Having the drive and motivation coming from within you, being passionate and loving what you are doing will show in your work and your readers and audience will be able to sense that.

When you choose to write about a niche that you actually love or you are passionate about then it will come out naturally from you and the process will be a lot smoother and enjoyable.

If you are enjoying what you are doing, then being able to maintain your blog and consistently put out good contents for your readers will become second nature to you, instead of having a heavy weight that you have to carry all the time if you don't enjoy the process.

A common reason why there are blogs that die down after months or just few years of having them is because the bloggers themselves lack the motivation and the drive to write anymore blog posts because the topic doesn't excite them anymore or they ran out of ideas about the topic because they have limited knowledge or expertise on the subject.

That's why finding the right niche for your blog is so much more than what is popular, what is trending, or what everyone else is doing. It is more about you, evaluating yourself, the things you love to do or what you are passionate about.

Stay Focus On A Specific Niche. By all means, try to stay away from a general topic blog. Meaning, try to stay away from having a blog with no clear concise topic. With a general blog, a blogger usually just blog about whatever topic comes to mind.

It's been proven time and time again that most people cannot please everybody. If you try to cater to everybody, there is a good chance that you ended up catering to nobody.

Come to think of it, if one day you are writing about makeup and beauty products, and then the next blog post is about crafting, then another post is about animals. There is obviously no clear, concise blog topic going on and this can be very confusing, scattered and all over the place, don't you think so too?

How do you think your audience would feel?

By doing this, there is a huge tendency that you are going to lose valuable loyal readers and followers and some may even un-follow or unsubscribe if they feel lost and confuse about what your blog is really about.

Granted, you may be interested in makeup, crafting, and animals, but your readers may not be all interested in the same topics combined as you are.

If you can find the right balance between what you love and what your readers love, then that would be the ideal case. You need to find that common ground in your blog that you and your readers can virtually meet and be able to enjoy each other's presence discussing a specific topic that you all are passionate about and/or can relate to.

The more niche specific your blog is, the better chances you have of attracting highly targeted readers that are truly interested in most if not all of the blog posts that you will publish.

It is worth noting that having a specific-niche blog will attract specific readers that are most interested in your specific niche, therefore, your readers will ended up being a highly targeted audience, which means that majority of them will most likely re-visit your blog and read your future blog entries because they know exactly the type of contents you share, so the possibility that these readers will stick around, remain as followers, and looking forward to your upcoming blog posts are higher.

Blog Money-Making Opportunity Warning And Heads Up

Note: This chapter is not about how to make money with your blog, but rather a warning and a heads up about some money-making opportunities that currently exist that you have to be aware of in advance to preserve your blog's credibility.

As you indulge yourself in the blogosphere (the world of blogging) you might start to uncover different ways and opportunities that you can possibly monetize your blog. Really, there are bloggers that do make money with their blogs!

It is not unethical to think and consider about monetizing your blog at all. We all have bills to pay and we all somehow have to find means to pay them. Blogging takes a lot of your time and energy, it is reasonable that you may consider finding a way to monetize your blog somehow in order to keep going with this time-consuming hobby or activity.

Blogging these days is definitely growing and becoming more and more popular, not only to people who like to write personal informal documentation of their day to day living and experiences, but as well as for several different companies and businesses that embrace this effective online platform, blogging, that allows them to reach out to more potential customers and audience.

Blogging has definitely reached new heights as more and more businesses are warming up to the idea of blogging as an advertising medium for their products and services. More companies are utilizing blogs as an effective means to promote their products and services which then opens up various opportunities for bloggers to earn money with their blogs.

There are multiple different ways that you can monetize your blog, but this topic is beyond the scope of this book.

One way to monetize your blog (which I will lightly discuss in this chapter) is through sponsored posts in which you, as the blogger, will review or test certain products or services of companies or individuals and you create a dedicated blog post (per product or service) about your experience, test result, honest thoughts and opinions about the product or service. And in exchange for such exposure and publicity of their product or service, the company or individual who asked for such review or blog exposure will compensate you for your time and blog publication.

When the time comes that you own a blog and would later decide that you want to monetize it and you would like to tap into this growing form of advertising which is writing articles or blog posts that are sponsored or paid for, you may begin to uncover a lot of sponsored post opportunities from various businesses offering all kinds of different types of products and services. With the potential to make money, it is so easy and tempting to jump in to every opportunity that comes along, and just accept whatever topic comes in your way.

But as emphasized in the previous chapter, it is best to keep your blog focus on a specific niche. And try to avoid having a general blog which is writing about all kinds of different topics.

For instance, if your blog is about travel and then you came across an opportunity to write a review about gaming or medical products, are you then willing to accept such opportunities just to earn some dollars?

It is important to mention and make you aware that once you accept certain sponsored post and have such sponsored post published in your blog and paid for, you might be obliged to keep such post published in your blog indefinitely, but that solely depends on the agreement between you and the business who availed your blogging promotion services. If this is the case, then once you do, it is hard to undone.

To avoid having regrets later on, always try to be selective of any money-making deals that you take and accept. Make sure that everything stays in line with the overall long term vision of your blog. Filter out opportunities that are unrelated to your blog niche. So, accept paid posting with caution especially if it is off-topic to your blog.

As previously emphasized in this book, you should always try to retain specific niche for your blog. Therefore, only accept paid posts that are related to your niche, if possible.

Whenever you do decide to monetize your blog and allow sponsored posts published on it, you should only accept writing jobs and advertisings that would complement your existing topic and that your audience can use or benefit.

Back to the example above, if your blog is about travel, then it is definitely not a good idea to add a blog post that talk about online gaming, or surgery, etc. If you do this, your blog will definitely lost focus and these unrelated paid contents could possibly turn off your regular readers and followers.

Some of your readers may be forgiving and can tolerate minor off-topic blog posts once in a while, it is still a gamble for you to go that route. You may get away with it sometimes and still retain your readers loyalty and readership. But if you go off-topic with your blog posts way more than your readers can tolerate, then you could potentially lost followers, which I am sure not what you want.

The question is, are you willing to lose followers that you worked so hard acquiring just to earn few dollars by accepting unrelated sponsored posts? In trying to earn few dollars, you may be slowly if not abruptly harming your blog's reputation by accepting paid posts that are off-topic and unrelated to what your blog is all about.

You need to find the right balance between keeping the followers that you worked so hard acquiring and the making money opportunities that you want to implement in your blog. A blog with no audience and an advertising in your blog with no viewers are both ineffective. So proceed with caution.

For any sponsored posts that will meet your criteria and accept to blog about, you still have to be extra watchful with the frequency of paid posts versus your regular posts. Personally, I think a great ratio would be 1 is to 10. One paid post for every ten non-paid posts. It could either be higher or lower than 10 but the higher the non-paid posts in between paid post, the better.

Learn to be creative in adding paid posts in your blog because people are generally sensitive when it comes to any form of advertising, not just sponsored post but banner ads, pop-up ads, etc. You don't want to give your audience the impression that you just want to make money with your blog instead of providing value to them because once that trust is broken, it is hard to get it back.

For long term sake, if you want to retain your blog's reputation intact the whole time, it's good to reiterate and review your blog's goals and purpose, what topics are acceptable to you that you are willing to include in your write ups that your audience can tolerate but most importantly benefit from without harming your blog's reputation in the process.

Some unrelated and off-topic sponsored posts can be temptations waiting to happen because they can be easy money. Usually, all you need to do to complete a sponsored blog post task is gather your honest thoughts and opinions on specific product or service, put it on writing and publish it on your blog. Just remember that not all money is good money. Not all sponsored posts opportunities that comes your way may be suitable for your blog. As mentioned, once posted, it is hard to undone it. Learn to say no, don't get pressured, remember, it is your blog and it's your blog's reputation that will be on the line. Ultimately, the decision is all up to you, and this is just a heads up.

Although, making money with your blog is beyond the scope of this book, I am covering this chapter specifically to emphasize on the importance of not losing focus on your overall blog vision and try to stay focus with your blog niche without derailing to other topics just so you can earn some money.

I wished that someone had warned me about this when I first started blogging, but then again, I have learned my lesson the hard way.

One of my earlier blogs had some paid posts. I wasn't really aware of the consequences of what I was doing, saying yes to some paid blog post opportunities that had nothing to do with my overall blog niche. For lack of a better word, I feel like some of those unrelated paid posts ruined the main focus of the blog. With that said, consider yourself warned as there are money-making opportunities out there for blogs.

Later on in your blogging journey, whenever you will decide to monetize and accept some paid blog posts, hope you will remember this book and try to pick and choose, and don't just blindly say yes to every sponsored post opportunities to get quick bucks that will probably not last very long in your pocket, but could potentially put a permanent dent or a scar on your blog.

Whatever sponsored post you take, make sure that you believe in the product or service 100 percent. Preserve your integrity, be selective. If you found no product nor service to review that suits your blog, then so be it. The most important thing is that you stay credible. Think long term.

Branding Your Blog And Other Online Platforms

DISCLAIMER: There are some portions of this chapter that contains excerpt from my other book, How To Make A YouTube Channel. So if you happen to read that book prior to this one, that's why some paragraphs may sound alike because of trying to explain the same topics without the inconvenience of referring you or sending you to another book. It seems more convenient for the reader if I just insert such information in this book directly.

If you are serious about your blog and where it's going in the near future and you have long term goals for your blog, then you might need to consider properly branding your blog right from the start.

Niche Specific Blog Naming Convention. When naming your blog, I highly suggest that you think of a name that will suits well basing on the type of contents or articles that you will write and publish on your blog. For example, if you are planning to publish all about crafting, then you might want to think of a name that by just reading the brand name itself, people will be able to kind of tell that you have a crafting blog.

One benefit of doing this is that it will help some potential readers and blog visitors, when they read your brand name (as indicated in your domain name), be enticed to click on your URL link to check out your blog entries just because they are aware of themselves being interested in crafting and they figured your blog niche basing on your brand name / domain name.

One thing can lead to another. A potential blog reader reading your branding somewhere, got interested and ended up in your blog because of it, and later becomes a loyal follower.

Your Name As The Brand Name. Some bloggers resort to just using their real names as the name of their blogs. Many bloggers do attain success with their blogs using their real names as the brand, and them as the face of the brand.

But if you are not a famous person at the start, using your name may not be so recognizable to majority of the people so it will be harder in the beginning to try to make people aware what your blog is all about, and what type of content you have in your blog.

Although, overtime as you get more exposure and gain more readers then there will be people that will be able to recognize your name in relation to your blog.

There are definitely great advantages of using your name as a brand name, especially when you also use it as a domain name for your blog or website. One obvious advantage is self branding. Every time you market your brand, you are marketing yourself. The more you market and expose your brand, the more your name become known and familiar to many. With great exposure of your name as a brand, more and more people will likely become familiar with you, and if you have history of great quality blog posts, products and/or services, then chances are, people who are familiar with your name/brand will likely try and utilize your new products and services as well.

But not everyone who has a blog has this goal of being recognize by their name. Some bloggers prefer to use niche specific naming convention (as discussed earlier in this chapter) and remain anonymous when it comes to their personal identity.

As noted earlier, if you decide to use your name as your brand, then people will not be able to tell right away what your channel is all about. Whereas if you decide on a brand name using the niche specific naming convention method, some people will be able to make that instant decision after reading your branding if they are interested in your blog topic or not.

Disadvantage of Using Your Name As The Brand. As your blog grows and develops, it may someday turn into a real business. A business with your real name attached to it.

The only main pitfall of using your name as a brand is that it will be harder for you to sell your business (if you decide to do so in the future) since you are currently carrying the same name personally. If someone buys your business, then you are most likely obligated to give them the right to use your name as well, if you are selling your business with its current name.

There's a possibility that the business buyer will consider rebranding but the likelihood of them doing so might be slim because they will have to start from scratch promoting a new brand. Most businesses are well aware that building a brand takes time and advertising money in order for people to recognize the name and the overall branding.

With that said, the business buyer will most likely keep the existing brand name, which in this case is your real name, since it is already an established brand at that point in time and existing customers already built that trust associated with the brand name.

In case of the business buyer rebranding and decided not to keep your name, such changes could potentially detach the trust and connection that were already established with the old brand because of unfamiliarity not only in the new branding but the new owners and management.

When someone buys your business, you normally will have less or no longer have any control to the operation and reputation of the company, and what the company will become. And that would be hard losing control of when your real name is still attach to it.

Therefore, before you fully commit to the idea of using your real name as the brand, this selling-the-business issue is definitely something to think about if ever you have future plans to sell your blog or business. Because if you do plan to sell, then it would probably be better if you don't have to sell it with your real name as the business name or brand.

These branding decisions are entirely up to you. You have to make these type of decision depending on your vision, goals and plans for your blog.

Besides, this topic may be way far off the main topic of this book which is how to create a blog, but I think it's worth thinking about in advance because although it is hard to predict the future of your blog, success is apparent if you put a lot of time, effort, hard work into producing quality blog contents and maintain consistency in your blog postings. If you have to think about the future of your blog now, might as well look at the bright side of things.

On the other hand, if you think that selling your blog or business is not an option that you would ever consider, then there is hardly a reason to worry about using your name as the brand for your blog.

Utilizing Your Brand In Other Online Platforms. When it comes to other online venues, it will be best if you stay consistent with your branding including all social media platforms like Facebook, Google+, etc so that people will be able to recognize you easily as one and the same individual or entity, and your followers don't have to second guess if it's you or not.

Across multiple online platforms, there are viewers that tend to assume that since it's the same brand name, they will assume that they are owned or operated by the same person or entity, and if that is not the case with your website or blog and your social media profiles then this could possibly create confusion, which ones are yours and which ones are not.

Protected Words. A word of caution though, when thinking of a name or brand for your blog, you have to take into consideration that there are protected words, proprietary words and trademarks therefore you cannot use these words as part of your brand name. For example, you cannot put the word Google in your blog name as part your branding, for instance YourChosenBlogNameGoogle, because the term

Google is a protected brand name. So you have to be mindful of these stuff while brainstorming for a name for your blog.

Having A Domain Name For Your Blog

Your Blog's Domain Name Is Part Of Branding. When it comes to branding, you should try to be consistent in all avenues of your blog including your blog's domain name.

Having the right domain name for your blog is like having the right TV commercial for your product. In other words, domain name matters. It carries the reputation of your company, business or organization. Domain name is just as important as your blog's contents. Domain name is just as important as a company logo. It carries your brand and eventually it will become a part of your overall branding and will carry your business reputation as well.

Generic Domain Name and/or Blogspot URL Address. There are cases that you can obtain a generic domain name for your blog therefore you don't have to worry about registering a domain name and paying for the registration fee annually.

A blog with a generic domain name usually indicates that you are currently using a free blogging platform like Blogger.com or WordPress.com and utilizing their server space to store all your blog data for free.

In case of using Blogger blogging platform (Blogger.com), the generic domain name or URL address of your blog will be in this format, YourChosenBlogName.blogspot.com

In case of using WordPress.com blogging platform, the generic domain name or URL address of your blog will be in this format, YourChosenBlogName.wordpress.com

When you sign-up for a blog with Blogger.com you will be prompted in the beginning of the blog creation process to setup your generic domain name, YourChosenBlogName.blogspot.com.

You can use this generic domain name to promote your blog but the problem with it is that you don't really own the domain name. Later on, whenever you decide to switch blogging platforms (for example from Blogger to WordPress) then you cannot carry along with you your YourChosenBlogName.blogspot.com domain since this generic domain name only works with the Blogger blogging platform.

I highly suggest not to keep using the generic domain name even if you are hosting your blog for free. For one, it looks very unprofessional. For two, it screams free. For three, you will be spending months, if not years, promoting your blog and if you are promoting a generic domain name then you will have no permanent ownership of it and sometime in the future when you decide to transfer from one blogging platform to another, the generic domain name will stay with the blogging platform that provided it for you. Therefore, all the years of hard work promoting your generic domain name will be for nothing.

Custom Domain Name. Having a custom domain name for your blog means that you registered a URL address for your blog via a domain name registrar which you can easily find one online.

Whatever brand name (as discussed in previous chapter) you decided on for your blog, I highly suggest that you register the same brand name as your blog's domain name or URL address in a format like this www.YourChosenBlogName.com

Consider checking a domain registration website or a registrar to check the availability of your chosen brand name, www.YourChosenBlogName.com. And if you have the budget, you might want to register such domain name, if its available, while it's available.

If you are either serious about blogging or having a custom domain name is part of your future plan, then you might have to consider looking at domain name registration today in order to lock it in and you will have uniformity when it comes to your branding. In fact, your custom domain name will help build your credibility as a brand.

But if you don't have plans or the desire to maintain a custom domain name for your blog, then you can just ignore and not worry about registering a custom domain name, save the yearly fees, and just utilize the free generic domain name (discussed above). Although, I would not advise that you go this route, but this decision is entirely up to you.

Once registered, start using your blog's custom domain name right away and use it to promote your blog so that any effort of marketing and advertising that you do with your blog using your custom domain name, www.YourChosenBlogName.com, will not be wasted because you own it, and you carry it with you from one platform to another whenever you need to switch blogging platforms sometime in the future.

Another reason why you have to consider registering a custom domain name now rather than later is that changing your blog's branding to accommodate a custom domain name later on will be a lot harder especially if you already built a huge following using your old branding.

Unpredictable scenarios do happen to some bloggers, who ended up growing bigger than they originally envisioned, and they have to face the reality of formalizing their online presence to keep up with the growth of their blog and turn it into a viable business entity. Having your own custom domain name is an important part of online business. It represents your online location, your virtual address.

For awareness sake, I am mentioning this custom domain name registration here so that you will have these possible scenarios laid out to you in advance, so that you won't ended up being on a situation, sometime in the future, when proper branding with corresponding custom domain name for your blog is something that you wanted all along, and then sometime in the future you grow exponentially in your online presence more than you anticipated and when you finally decide to check the availability of the domain name at a future time rather than now, it might be too late for you to register a domain name if someone already registered it before you.

Having a custom domain name for your blog is not something that you need to have at all, nor is it required, nor is it necessary, but I'm just mentioning this now to give you an idea of what could possibly happen in the future that you might not even thought of.

One thing to note though is that there is a cost involve yearly to maintain a custom domain name. Depending on the registrar, it can cost you anywhere from $10 to $35 per year. Plus, there are additional fees associated with it like if you want to add privacy service in the registered custom domain name so that your personal information like name, address, contact information, will not be publicly viewable as the registered owner of the domain name.

Ultimately, registering a domain name are all up to you to decide, depending on your vision, your goal, and what you want to achieve with regards to your online presence both the present time and in the future.

In my case, personally, this is what I usually do, before I create a blog, I check the availability of the domain name first because I don't like the idea of putting too much time, energy and effort promoting and growing a brand name when I don't own the domain name on it.

Generic Domain Name Versus Custom Domain Name. So what are the advantages and disadvantages of having your own custom domain name instead of using the generic domain name?

First and for most, I personally think that there is no major disadvantages of having your own custom domain name, except for the cost of maintaining or keeping the domain name registered in your name year after year.

But regardless of whether you own a custom domain name, or you are using a generic domain name or generic URL address, you are still going to take the time and effort to promote your blog, either way. And this is when the main advantage of having your own custom domain name comes in.

If you own your own custom domain name for your blog, then you are promoting your own brand.

Whenever you decide to change or switch from one blogging platform to another, your custom domain name will remain the same because you can continue to use your own custom domain name regardless of what blogging platform you are using. Therefore, all the time and effort you spent over the years promoting your custom domain name will not be wasted because you will always have the same domain name that will point to your blog, even if you change servers, hosting companies, or blogging platforms.

Unlike a generic domain name which will stay with the current blogging platform that owns the generic domain name. Therefore, the generic domain name (YourChosenBlogName.blogspot.com) that you obtained from Blogger.com is not-transferable to another platform. Any effort that you do/did promoting your generic domain name will be down the drain.

Back to custom domain name, the only time that your effort promoting it will be wasted completely is when you decide to overhaul your whole entire online presence including your brand name, so then you will need to change and register a new custom domain name to match your new brand name. If you do this, then you have to start from the ground up promoting your new brand which includes your new custom domain name.

In more technical sides, getting rid of your promoted custom domain name also means losing all the search engine rankings that your old domain name already achieved, and losing all the back links that you already built over time. (Note: I will not cover about search engine rankings and back links since these are beyond the scope of this book).

Choosing A Blogging Platform - Self-Hosted or Free-Hosted Blog

When choosing a blogging platform, first you have to consider whether you want to pay for hosting a blog or use a free hosting blogging platform.

Web Hosting Service. Paying for web hosting means paying for a data server space in order for you to be able to store all of your blog's digital data files that are associated with your blog contents which include all your blog posts' data files, text documents files, photos and images files, music and audio files, video files, etc.

Think of a data server being similar to your computer's hard drive, being a virtual memory storage, with the capability to store your digital or computer files.

The main difference between your computer's hard drive and a remote data server is that your desktop or laptop computer's hard drive memory is a private and standalone memory storage unless you have it connected to a network with file sharing capability. With all the private personal files stored in your computer hard drive, you can't just let the world have access to it, do you?

On the other hand, a remote data server will function as a web host that is capable of storing digital files just like a computer hard drive but you can easily access such files through the internet because you can set it up to connect to the world wide web (WWW) network.

The decision whether you have to pay for a web hosting service monthly or not depends on your answer to the question, do you want a self-hosted blog or a free-hosted blog?

Self-Hosted Blog. If your answer to the question above is self-hosted blog, then one very popular blogging software or platform that is capable of supporting a paid hosting blog is WordPress at WordPress.org website.

To have a self-hosted blog using WordPress, you need to find a service provider that offers web hosting service (as explained earlier in this chapter). But before you avail such service, you need to verify that their web hosting server supports the WordPress software or blogging platform. If it does, you can then install WordPress software in your hosting account so that you can go ahead and start working on setting up your blog.

Some web hosting companies may already have integrated the WordPress blogging software in their system, if this is the case then you just have to enable or initiate connection of the software within your web hosting control panel (customer account) in order for you to get started setting up your blog.

Free-Hosted Blog. If your answer to the question above is free-hosted blog then a very popular blogging platform that offers free-hosted blogging capability is Blogger at Blogger.com

Blogger is a web-based blogging platform which means that you don't have to install any software in your computer in order to setup or maintain your blog. All you need to do initially is sign up for a Blogger account (which will be discussed further in a later chapter) in order to have access to the platform.

While log-in to your Blogger account, you will have the ability to setup and create a blog (which will be discussed further in a later chapter).

Since the Blogger platform is a web-based platform, you need an internet connection to access the platform in order for you to setup and create a blog, post a blog post, or maintain your blog.

With free-hosted blogs like the ones provided by Blogger, you don't need to avail a web hosting service and pay for a monthly fee for it. With free-hosted blog, your blog contents' digital files will be hosted or stored for free in a remote data server owned by Blogger.com

Difference Between WordPress.org And WordPress.com
You might be wondering what is the difference between the blogging platforms available at WordPress.org and WordPress.com?

As explained earlier in this chapter, the blogging platform available at WordPress.org is capable of having your blog being self-hosted.

On the other hand, the blogging platform available at WordPress.com is similar to Blogger in such a way that it allows you to have a free-hosted blog and you can obtain a free generic domain name for your blog with format YourChosenBlogName.wordpress.com

To be totally transparent, I, personally, never used the free-hosted blogging platform at WordPress.com. One deciding factor for me not to use it was due to the fact that I will not be allowed to monetize the blog like I could with a Blogger blog. Although, I didn't plan to monetize my blog right away, I wanted to have the option to monetize later on if I want to do so in the future, which I could by using Blogger.

For the remainder of this book, I will primarily focus on discussing about Blogger.com (not WordPress.com) when talking about free-hosted blogs.

Now that you have a general idea regarding what is the difference between a self-hosted blog (like WordPress at WordPress.org) and a free-hosted blog (like Blogger at Blogger.com), you are left with a decision to make. Which option would you choose as the home base for the blog that you want to create?

In the next two chapters, we will further explore both WordPress and Blogger blogging platforms. Hopefully, these chapters will help you make a sound decision which blogging platform is right for you that will meet your needs and wants.

WordPress Overview / Self-Hosted Blogging Platform

WordPress at WordPress.org is by far one of the most popular, if not the most popular blogging platform for self-hosted blog.

As explained in previous chapter, you need a web hosting account in order to setup a WordPress blog.

Advantages Of Using Self-Hosted WordPress Blogging Platform. One great thing about having a self-hosted WordPress blog is that you have complete control of your blog. The fact that all your blog data files are stored in a web hosting server that you paid for does gives you some kind of assurance that no one can take your blog away from you unless you don't pay the monthly hosting fee!

With WordPress, you have access to premium plug-ins that are usually not available to use on free-hosted blogs.

There are wide variety of WordPress themes or templates available in the market both paid and free templates, so you have plenty of options to find the right design and layout for your blog however you want it to look and feel.

Using ready-to-use templates is perfect for you if you don't want to mess around nor have the technicality to do HTML and CSS coding. For non-techie bloggers, having all these WordPress themes to choose from is totally time-saving, and cost-effective because hiring a professional web designer or front-end web developer to customize your blog can be very costly.

Considering both paid and free templates, there are literally several hundreds if not thousands of WordPress themes in several different type of industries like business, fashion, food, etc. The only problem you are left with is having to choose one among all of these choices!

WordPress blogs are known for its professional looking themes or templates. This is one of the reason why WordPress is hugely popular because we all want to give the best impression to our audience. With several professional looking themes available for WordPress blogs, it is not hard to have a blog that will look visually appealing and impressive.

If using the WordPress blogging platform is so robust, widely used and currently dominating the blogging industry then why even consider another blogging platform? Why even consider free-hosted blogging platform like Blogger? Some answers as to why will be covered in full details in the next chapter.

But first, let me find some valid points to understand that having a self-hosted blog using WordPress may not be for everyone.

Disadvantages Of Using Self-Hosted WordPress Blogging Platform. Honestly, I can't think of major disadvantages of using a self-hosted WordPress blogging platform. I do, however, have few concerns which I will explain shortly after this, please keep reading.

As explained in previous chapter, to have a self-hosted blog using WordPress blogging platform, you will need a web hosting service which is not free. That means you need to pay for the monthly web hosting fee which can cost you anywhere from $3 to $20 for basic web hosting packages. It doesn't sound like a lot but it is still a recurring cost, a cost you will have to pay for as long as you want to keep your blog running and operating.

Monthly fee adds up and if your blog is not generating revenue then all these recurring costs will ended up being expenses, no profit.

What I find unforgiving is any possibility of unforeseen circumstances that may prevent you from paying your monthly web hosting dues that can then cause you to lose access to your web hosting account which is basically the lifeline of your blog. Worst case scenario, due to non-payment, the web hosting company could decide to free up the memory storage that your blog files occupies and this could mean that all your blog's data files will be deleted in their system or server to free up memory space and therefore will make your blog virtually non-existent. And if you have no backup available to retrieve all your blog data?

So, who says that no one can take away your blog from you when you are self-hosted? The web hosting company can! Or you can by not paying the monthly dues.

Paying for web hosting maybe minimal cost to you but if by any chance you forget to pay on time, you could potentially lose your blog at some point because your blog is composed of a bunch of digital files, stored in the data server that you rented from a web hosting company, taking up memory space. Just like renting a house, if you don't pay your monthly rent then your landlord could kick you out. To prevent this from happening, you can usually setup an automatic payments. If available, always opt-in for automatic renewals instead of manual.

Another concern that I can think of is that although there are hundreds of WordPress templates (both paid and free) that are available in the market, which was previously mentioned in this book as a great advantage of using WordPress blogging platform, but not all of these templates are in responsive format or mobile-ready.

A responsive format website or blog automatically adjust depending on the size of the device' screen or what type of device your blog or website is being viewed on.

With the fast-growing popularity of smart phones and other handheld devices including tablets, and the growing number of users utilizing mobile devices to access the internet, such usage patterns suggest that browsing online with mobile devices are just getting stronger.

Therefore, you cannot ignore not having a responsive format and/or a mobile-ready blog to keep up with this growing trend which could potentially become the new norm in the not-so-distant future.

With that said, you have to seriously consider that some of your potential blog readers may be using mobile devices instead of computers to browse your blog. If you are not, then you could potentially eliminate more than half of your potential readers. Nowadays, you almost need a mobile-friendly and/or responsive format blog so that you can accommodate all your readers regardless what device they are using.

Although, there are hundreds of WordPress templates to date, most likely not all of them are mobile-ready. And in order to stay current, and most importantly, to be able to accommodate a growing demographic of mobile device users, who are also your potential blog audience, you are left with not all hundreds of templates to choose from.

The not-so-obvious concern of going self-hosted route of blogging is security concerns. Self-hosted blogs are sometimes vulnerable to hacking and needing security patches to keep your account secure and avoid your files and web hosting account from being access by those who have nothing else to do but mess around with other people's property (like your blog).

It's like renting a house, the homeowner may be able to provide you a safe sturdy home to live, but the homeowner have little control over scenarios like an intruder getting into your home. However, you, as the house occupant, can prevent this from happening by installing security systems and locking doors and windows.

Blogger Overview / Free-Hosted Blogging Platform

When it comes to free-hosted blogging platform, Blogger at Blogger.com, in my opinion, is on top of the list.

There are several other free-hosted blogging platforms available like WordPress.com (not WordPress.org) but this book will primarily cover free-hosted Blogger blogging platform.

In the previous chapter, I discussed about self-hosted blog using WordPress blogging platform (at WordPress.org) and pointed out some of the advantages as well as some minor concerns or disadvantages of using the software. Having read that, if you feel that you are still open to consider other options aside from self-hosted WordPress blog then keep reading as this chapter will discuss more about free-hosted blog using Blogger blogging platform and explore some of the advantages and disadvantages of using one.

As mentioned earlier, Blogger is a web-based blogging platform which means that you don't need to install any software in your computer in order to setup and create a blog, construct a blog post, or maintain your blog. All you basically need is to sign-up for a Blogger account (which will be discussed more in the next chapter) and then perform the initial setup and the creation process of your blog (which will be discussed in a later chapter).

You do need an internet connection in order to access this web-based platform and be able to perform any blogging activities like publishing a blog post, template customization, blog maintenance, etc.

If someone actually told you never to use a free-hosted blogging platform like Blogger, ask why. Also ask when was the last time did he/she actually use the platform, chances are years. Perhaps the naysayer just blindly saying not to use the platform without any solid experience of actually using it recently. Also, there might be some people that simply echo what other people are saying, not to use free-hosted blog, without really knowing the reasoning behind it.

In this chapter, I will discuss more about the advantages and the disadvantages of using free-hosted Blogger blogging platform (at Blogger.com) so that you have some overview of the pros and cons of using it which will hopefully help you decide to either go with self-hosted (as discussed in previous chapter) or free-hosted.

There are some great positive changes in the Blogger platform in recent years.

I have personally used the Blogger blogging platform for several years. I witnessed firsthand some positive changes, updates, upgrades, improvements, and/or enhancements in the platform. For me, I feel that the platform is definitely heading in the right direction since they put so much work, effort, and time making the platform better and better as years go by.

I have nothing against WordPress, I think it is an awesome blogging platform. It is the most popular blogging platform to date and it is versatile and customizable. Some of the pros and cons of using self-hosted WordPress blogging platform were discussed in previous chapter.

In this chapter, I will focus primarily on the free-hosted Blogger blogging platform and examine the pros and cons of using one mostly based on my personal experience of using one for several years.

<u>Not All Free-Hosted Blogging Platforms Are Created Equal.</u> Some people may tell you never to use free service, blogging platform included, reason being is that it is unprofessional and amateurish. Just because it is free does not mean it is a bad thing!

Come to think of it, the YouTube platform is free to use as well, but content creators from all walks of life from all over the world flock to YouTube and utilize the platform day in and day out. People utilize the YouTube platform not because it's free but because of its capability and its functionality.

One of my reason why I use Blogger is not because it's free but more so because of its capabilities and functions.

If the blogging platform meets all your criteria and very capable of everything that you need and want in a blogging platform, then why not consider it.

Personally, I don't just use any free blogging platform available out there, I use Blogger. Granted, there are a lot of free blogging platforms out there but I would not even consider using most of them and I have my reasons, which I will discuss shortly after this.

For me, I look beyond the word free and actually look at the platform itself. I look not only its capabilities and functionalities but most importantly who is behind the blogging software, which in the case of Blogger is owned by Google, the same company that actually owns YouTube (as of this writing). With a big reliable company behind the blogging software, even though it is free to use, I feel confident that in the next several months or years, my blog will not mysteriously fade and disappear because I am quite confident that the company (Google) will not be out of business!

I highly consider the long term lifespan and the future of my blog that is why when I was considering free blogging platform I went past the word free and considered the company behind the blogging software in order for me to have some kind of assurance that my blog will remain activate and running for years to come.

Even if you are highly confident that a blogging company that offers free blogging platform will remain in business for a long time, there's still risk involve, like the possibility of losing your blog. There are no guarantees. It is one of those decision that you have to make at the beginning of your blog creation process if you are willing to move forward using a free blogging platform and be willing to take that risk.

Ultimately, you have no control over the operations and services of the private company that owns the blogging platform. Any decision that they make in the future with regards to their platforms is their decision to make, and as an end-user that is using the platform for free or at no charge, you can be in a vulnerable position. The risk is there, so you have to be willing to take the risk of you possibly being affected by any future decisions they may make that could potentially cause you to lose your blog. If so, hopefully you have some kind of backup then.

Having said that, that's why I find it so important to assess the company behind the free blogging platform before making a long time commitment to use their platform for free for several years. Doing so will hopefully minimize the risk of losing your blog that you will put so much time and effort building.

I have some experiences using free platforms only to find out that the company either sold their business, eliminate the platform or certain feature in their website, discontinue offering the free platform, etc. which caused me to lose my platforms' accounts or profiles entirely. A company deciding to discontinue servicing a free platform can be due to several reasons like not having enough budget to keep the platform going, there's not enough users utilizing the platform, the company has no way to monetize the platform therefore it is becoming an expense to the company, or the platform is not-profitable and not generating any income (because it is free!), etc.

Although, majority of companies do give their end-users a thoughtful warning notice or heads up whenever they will be closing or discontinuing a service or a platform for good in the not-so-distant future. And most company would give their end-users some kind of ultimatum email notifications that they need to export, backup, transfer files before such date in order to avoid losing any files that they may have in their system that the users cannot afford to lose. That is if you, as an end-user, catch the warning email notification that they sent out and not have it slip away or buried undetected with all the junk emails that most of us receive in our inbox on a daily basis.

Even if you did catch the warning notice, you still have to go through the hassle of saving and backing up all your digital files that are stored in their system, maybe you need to perform file transfers, downloading, exporting, etc. in an effort to save or retrieve your files. It can be a hassle to go through all these to avail a free blogging platform.

For peace of mind, it is definitely best to look closely into the company behind the free-hosted blogging platform.

Free Blog Templates. Blogger provides some free user-friendly ready-to-use blog templates that are also customizable.

The layout customization interface is easy-to-use with drag and drop functionality so you don't need to learn or mess around with HTML and CSS coding to customize your blog's layout and widget arrangements or placements.

But at the same time, you also have the option to access the HTML and CSS codes of your chosen blog's template for customization, if you desired to do so, so it is quite versatile.

The template customization interface can be used by both non-techie blogger and tech-savvy blogger.

But unlike WordPress templates, there's not a lot of Blogger blog templates available to choose from but whatever is available, you do have the option to edit the appearance and further customize the layout (which will be further discussed in a later chapter) to your liking and needs.

Widgets or Gadgets. There are good selection of widgets or gadgets that you can use for free and be able to use it by simply picking and choosing in the widget library/listing in order to add to your blog.

Using the HTML widget, you can also insert other widgets from outside sources, just copy-and-paste the code inside the HTML widget in order to add such widget to your blog.

Mobile-Friendly Format. With the exponential rise of mobile users in recent years, it is almost critical and compulsory that your blog or website are mobile-friendly.

Most, if not all, of the new blog templates provided by Blogger to use for free can be enabled as mobile-friendly. At your Blogger user interface, you can enable the mobile-friendly option, if it's not automatically enabled at your end.

It is important to point out that Google search engine favors mobile-friendly websites and blogs nowadays as more and more users access the internet through their mobile devices including smart phones, and tablets, etc. So with Blogger providing mobile-friendly version of your blog, your blog is already ahead of the game.

Generic Domain Name and Custom Domain Name. During the initial blog creation process using Blogger platform, you will acquire a generic domain name or a Blogspot URL address for your blog in this format, YourChosenBlogName.blogspot.com, but don't worry because you can easily rename your blog if you decide to do so later on. And if you don't like using the generic domain name, no worries because you will not be stuck with it if you don't want to.

You can register your own custom domain name for your blog and have it setup later to point to your Blogger blog so that it will be formatted like this, www.YourChosenBlogName.com which I am sure everyone will agree will look and sound more professional, and it doesn't scream free!

Registering your own custom domain name is a separate service that you will have to pay for. You can either register your domain name through a registrar of your choice, or you can register through Blogger / Google by simply clicking a link within your Blogger user-interface to get a custom domain name.

With Blogger platform, rebranding is a breeze. In major circumstance that you have to change your custom domain name in order to accommodate your new brand name, you can easily remove the domain pointer of your old custom domain name that is pointing at your Blogger blog's generic domain name, and have your new custom domain name point to it.

In a possible worst case scenario in which you are unable to pay for your custom domain name registration fee (www.YourChosenBlogName.com) and you lost it, luckily with Blogger platform, you will not lost your blog and all the digital files associated with your blog because of it, simply switch back to using your generic domain name YourChosenBlogName.blogspot.com and your blog will be accessible again while you work out the issue with your custom domain name.

Integration With Other Google-Owned Platforms. One very good thing about Blogger blogging platform being owned by Google is that Blogger is conveniently integrated with other Google-owned platforms including Google website, Google+, YouTube, Google AdSense, etc. If that is not an advantage, then that must be a privilege or a luxury feature! And because they are integrated internally within the Google system, you can easily connect and associate your Blogger blog with these other Google-owned platforms, which I like a lot! Most of which can be done with few mouse-clicks, easy breezy.

You even have the option to use Google+ comment feature for your Blogger blog or chose to keep the comment feature that comes with your Blogger blog's template. As of this writing, you can even switch back and forth which comment feature you would rather use.

Web Hosting Security. When you are using free-hosted Blogger blogging platform it means that all your blog contents and entries digital files are stored somewhere in a remote server owned by Blogger.com and/or Google. You hardly have to worry about hacking vulnerability, security issues at your end since Blogger and/or Google take care of the Blogger platform and server security at their end.

More About The Blogger Blogging Platform. After reading some of the pros and cons of using the free-hosted Blogger blogging platform (as discussed in this chapter) and you would like to explore more about it and how it works, then the next four chapters are dedicated to setting up and working with Blogger.

Signing Up For A Blogger Account And Creating A Blog With Blogger

DISCLAIMER: There are some portions of this chapter that contains excerpt from my other book, How To Make A YouTube Channel. So if you happen to read that book prior to this one, that's why some paragraphs may sound alike because of trying to explain the same topics without the inconvenience of referring you or sending you to another book. It seems more convenient for the reader if I just insert such information in this book directly.

Blogger Account. In order to create a new blog using the free-hosted Blogger blogging platform, all you have to do is go to Blogger.com website. As of this writing, when you sign-up for a Blogger account, you will most likely be directed to Google because Blogger is owned by Google, and majority of their online platforms including Blogger, YouTube, Google+ are integrated with Google and they let you access these different platforms, owned by Google, using just one Google account.

So if you already have an existing Google account, then you should be able to use such account to login to Blogger.com website. All you have to do then is go to Blogger.com website and login using your current Google account.

Owning One Blog Versus Multiple Blogs. As of this writing, by using your Google account to login to the Blogger website, you should be able to create more than one blog, if you desired.

The reason for possibly creating more than one blog is explained in earlier chapter (What To Blog About) in cases where you want to write blog posts that are not on the same niche and you want a separate blog for each niche. For example, you want to create a crafting blog, and another blog for dieting. Since crafting articles and dieting articles seems too far apart topic-wise to be in one blog, this is one possibility why you may consider creating two blogs instead of one.

But if you are just starting out, and this is your very first blog and you have never done this before, I highly suggest that you focus on just one blog, therefore create just one blog for now.

Having one blog alone will require a lot of time and work already, two blogs at the same time means double the work for you. You need to be able to maintain both blogs without exhausting and overwhelming yourself. If you ever decide with two blogs instead of one, you have to know that both blogs will independently require your time, attention, contents, promotions, and hard work.

For starters, it would be best to start with just one blog. Get yourself familiar with the platform, the interface and how things works, learn and get accustomed with the whole process until you master or feel at ease with the whole thing.

You can always create another blog later on using the same Blogger account whenever you feel that you can handle running two blogs simultaneously without sacrificing the quality of your blog entries.

Create Your Blogger Blog. Once you are logged into the Blogger.com website, you can then create a new blog. To do so, click the New Blog button, as of this writing, currently located in the upper-left corner of the web page. You will then be directed to a pop-up page that will ask you for some details of the blog that you want to create including the title of your blog, the generic domain name of your blog (with format YourChosenBlogName.blogspot.com), and then choose a template among the ones that are provided, then click Create Blog button.

At this point, don't worry about setting up the custom domain name, if you registered one already. And don't worry too much about the template that you choose. Because later on you will have plenty of opportunity (whenever you are ready to do so) to setup the pointing of your custom domain name, and to customize or change the blog template, etc. In other words, you are not stuck permanently with your initial choices during the blog creation process.

Blogger Blog Layout Customization, Template Customization, Blog Settings

Blog Layout Customization. The Blogger layout user interface is a drag and drop feature. The Blogger blog layout is composed of blocks of widgets or gadgets that you can easily drag and drop therefore very easy to re-arrange, customize, and add sections (widget blocks) in your blog.

You can re-arrange the layout, add or remove widget / gadget to your existing blog template. To do so, click on either your blog title or the arrow-down button to reveal the pull-down menu, and then select or click Layout. From there, you can drag and drop the widget blocks to re-arrange, edit existing widgets, add new widgets by clicking Add A Gadget link, etc.

Blog Template Customization. You can choose to keep the blog template design that you originally picked in the beginning when you created the blog, or you can easily change it to another template of your choice that are available for free in the Blogger interface. To do so, click on either your blog title or the arrow-down button to reveal the pull-down menu, and then select or click Template. From there, you can explore and choose another template design available for free in the Blogger interface.

To further customize an existing Blogger blog template of your blog, go to your blog's pull-down menu and click Template. From there, click Customize button to customize existing template to your liking including background, blog width, body layout, etc. Click Advance link to change the default font sizes, font colors, etc.

Unfortunately, the templates available in the Blogger website don't always meet the design of the blog that you envisioned. You do however have an option to further customize and edit the existing HTML codes of your template as long as you do not remove any credits encoded in the original templates.

While in the Template interface, you have an access to the raw HTML code of the existing template by clicking the Edit HTML button. I highly advise that you don't mess with the HTML codes if you do not have an adequate knowledge of such coding language. But if you are comfortable customizing the blog template by further tweaking the HTML codes, then you do have this access to do so, but before you do, I strongly suggest that you backup your existing template first especially if you already have blog entries and sections or widgets added to your blog.

Third-Party Blogger Blog Templates. There are third-party websites that sell pre-made templates that are specifically designed to work with Blogger blogs. When you buy one of this pre-coded template, all you need to do is follow the installation instructions of the customized template that you purchased. These instructions are usually provided by the template seller. You should be able to change your existing template with the purchased template through the Template interface in Blogger.com website.

When you decide to buy a template for a Blogger blog from an independent third-party template seller, you need to be aware that some of the templates available for sale out there are not mobile-friendly.

Whereas, if you use a template provided by the Blogger website, most of the free templates that they provide, if not all, are mobile-friendly enabled.

As discussed in an earlier chapter, you need to have a mobile-friendly website or blog because the mobile-user demographic is rapidly increasing and you don't want your new blog to be on the obsolete side already.

More Blog Settings And Customization. While logged in to your Blogger account, you can further customize your blog or change the existing settings of your blog by going to your blog's pull-down menu, then click Settings. From there, you can add your blog description, change the domain name settings, edit blog posts and comments settings, email settings, language and formatting settings, add search preferences, and more.

Pointing Registered Custom Domain Name To Your Blogger Blog

Assuming that you already registered a custom domain name (discussed in an earlier chapter). You can then point your registered custom domain name to your existing Blogger blog which still have the generic domain name, YourChosenBlogName.blogspot.com. To point your custom domain name to your new blog, just click on either your blog title or the arrow-down button to reveal the drop-down menu, and then select or click Settings. Under Settings, click Basic. From there, you will be able to change the setting of your domain name under Publishing.

In the Publishing part of the page, click the link, + Setup a 3rd party URL for your blog, in order to point your custom domain name into your Blogger blog. In order to do this, make sure that you already registered a custom domain name with a domain registrar. While in the Publishing interface, click View Settings Instructions for further instructions.

You might need to contact your domain name registrar to help you setup the domain name pointing on their side of the server, if you don't know how to do it yourself.

IMPORTANT ONLINE SAFETY TIP: Your domain name registrar do not need access to your Blogger.com and/or Google account login information to perform the domain name pointing setup since you or a registrar staff can change the CNAME / DNS of your custom domain name at their end, in the registrar's server/platform. NEVER, in any circumstance, give your Google or Blogger username and password to your registrar when you contact them for help or assistance with pointing of your domain name.

Create Your First Blog Post With Blogger

After reading the three chapters prior to this one, I now assume that you already created your Blogger blog. With that said, it is time to get creative and construct your very first blog post!

To create your very first blog post, click the Create New Post button and you will be directed to the Editor interface and be able to encode or compose your blog post.

Alternatively, you can go to the pull-down menu of your blog and click the link Posts, you will then be directed to a page showing all your blog posts, if any, displayed by titles. From there, you can create a new blog post, simply click the New Post button in the page, you will then be directed to the Editor interface and be able to compose your blog post.

The Editor interface is very easy to use. If you are familiar using a word processor like MS Word, then using the Blogger's Editor interface should not be so foreign to you since it is quite similar, in fact, it is a lot simpler than a word processor.

The Editor interface is very user-friendly and a lot of the links and buttons are self-explanatory. You can insert or upload images and photographs. You can change the text font's colors, sizes, and characteristics (bold, italic, underline, or their combinations). You can insert hyperlinks. Change text alignments. Add numbered list or bullet list.

While in the Editor interface, you can switch back and forth between HTML mode or Compose mode.

The Compose mode is close to the same as a WYSIWYG (What-You-See-Is-What-You-Get) editor, or a word processor in which most of the features are user-friendly and self-explanatory.

The HTML mode allows you to edit the raw HTML codes of the blog post. The HTML mode will come handy if you are knowledgeable about HTML and want to further customize your post with coding. The HTML mode is also great if you want to embed videos from outside sources like YouTube.

While in the Editor interface, you will also have access to the settings of the current blog post that you are composing, and be able to add labels or tags, search description, and other post settings.

Once you are done writing and encoding your blog post, you can either click Save button to have it save as a draft, or you can click Publish button to have it posted as a live blog post.

To view your blog live, depending on your existing domain settings, either generic domain name or custom domain name setting, you can type in your internet browser's URL bar either the URL address http://YourChosenBlogName.blogspot.com or http://www.YourChosenBlogName.com

While in Blogger interface, you can alternatively view your live blog by clicking View Blog link or button.

Conclusion

The life of your blog and its longevity depends on you. The time and effort that you will put creating valuable contents for your blog will contribute to the overall success of your blog. The quality of blog posts that you publish and the consistency of your postings will help you build a loyal following and engaging readers.

The success of your blog will not happen overnight. Blogging is a journey, not a destination, one blog post at a time, so don't forget to have fun doing it. Try to make blogging a fun activity for you so that it will not feel like work. Remember, whenever you decide to move forward with blogging, then chances are you will be doing this for a long time, for as long as you want your blog to go on, maybe years, maybe a lifetime. So have fun with it, like I said, blogging is a journey, not a destination!

THANK YOU Message

I want to personally THANK YOU for reading this book. I hope that you found some valuable information in this book, and that you learned something useful and helpful by reading this book.

I need a favor from you!

If you found this book helpful and/or informative, please take a minute or two to leave me a review at Amazon, so that others will be able to find or discover this book as well and hopefully can benefit the same information discussed in this book.

I Have More BOOKS On The Way!!

Granted, this is NOT my last Book! I will be releasing more internet marketing strategies, making money online, online entrepreneurship, computer tips, etc. books in the near future. Don't miss any of it, simply sign-up to receive an email notification when I release a book. Sign-up form for my FREE newsletter available at www.DoingE.com

Sincerely,

Jazevox

https://www.amazon.com/author/jazevox

Made in the USA
Middletown, DE
28 June 2017